Presented to

～～～～～～～～～～～～～～～

by

～～～～～～～～～～～～～～～

on

～～～～～～～～～～～～～～～

GOD'S AMAZING CREATION

Tyndale House Publishers, Inc.
Carol Stream, Illinois

Visit Tyndale's website for kids at www.tyndale.com/kids.

Visit Group online at www.TheHandsOnBible.com and www.Group.com.

TYNDALE is a registered trademark of Tyndale House Publishers, Inc. The Tyndale Kids logo is a trademark of Tyndale House Publishers, Inc.

New Living Translation, *NLT*, and the New Living Translation logo are registered trademarks of Tyndale House Publishers, Inc.

Hands-On Bible, *Hands-On Bible Curriculum*, and the Group Publishing logo are registered trademarks of Group Publishing, Inc. The Hands-On Bible logo and the Hands-On Bible Curriculum logo are trademarks of Group Publishing, Inc.

God's Amazing Creation

Cover illustration copyright © by Paige Billin-Frye and Jane Yamada, represented by Portfolio Solutions, LLC.

Designed by Libby Dykstra

Content taken from *My First Hands-On Bible*, published in 2011 by Tyndale House Publishers, Inc.

My First Hands-On Bible Editorial Team: Sue Geiman, Erin Gwynne, Becki Manni, Joani Schultz, Betty Free Swanberg, Ali Thompson, Stephanie Rische, and Christine Yount Jones

My First Hands-On Bible Design Team: Jean Bruns, Daniel Farrell, and Randy Maid

My First Hands-On Bible Illustrators: Paige Billin-Frye and Jane Yamada, represented by Portfolio Solutions, LLC

My First Hands-On Bible Writers: Renée Gray-Wilburn, Marsha Maxfield Hall, Janna Kinner, Julie Lavender, Barbie Murphy, Karen Pennington, Janet R. Reeves, Elaine Ernst Schneider, Donna K. Simcoe, Courtney Walsh, and Dana Wilkerson

Scripture quotations are taken from the *Holy Bible*, New Living Translation, copyright © 1996, 2004, 2007 by Tyndale House Foundation. Used by permission of Tyndale House Publishers, Inc., Carol Stream, Illinois 60188. All rights reserved.

For manufacturing information regarding this product, please call 1-800-323-9400.

For information about special discounts for bulk purchases, please contact Tyndale House Publishers at csresponse@tyndale.com, or call 1-800-323-9400.

The Library of Congress has catalogued the hardcover edition as follows:

Bible. English. New Living Translation. Selections. 2011.
  My first hands-on Bible / [writers, Renée Gray-Wilburn et al.].
    p. cm.
  ISBN 978-1-4143-4830-8 (hc)
  I. Gray-Wilburn, Renée. II. Title.
  BS391.3.G73 2011
  220.9′505—dc22   2011005493

ISBN 978-1-4964-3750-1

Printed in China

25   24   23   22   21   20   19
7   6   5   4   3   2   1

Contents

How to Use These Bible Stories

Welcome to *God's Amazing Creation*! You and your child will explore God's Word together in fun and exciting ways as you read this book. You'll get to dig in to the Bible passages with fun activities as you read them, and then follow up your reading with simple activities that will make the Bible a part of your child's life.

Real Bible Text

God's Amazing Creation is special! We selected the New Living Translation (NLT) for its clarity for readers of all ages. Hearing Scripture in its true form will be a powerful experience for your child. Second Timothy 3:16 tells us, "All Scripture is inspired by God and is useful to teach us what is true and to make us realize what is wrong in our lives." With this book, your child can hear the God-inspired words of his book, the Bible.

We abridged the NLT passages to provide the most age-appropriate Scripture for preschoolers. You may find, though, that you occasionally come across a word that's unfamiliar to your child. If that's the case, stop and help your child understand what's happening in the part of the Bible you're reading. Or after you read a passage, ask your child to tell you what happened in the Bible story, and fill in any gaps in your own words.

Hands-On Activities

As you read, you'll come across colored handprints in the Bible text. When you see a handprint, stop reading and lead your child in the activity by the matching handprint. These are written for you to read aloud to your children. You'll get your child involved in the Bible passage through moving around, acting out, looking for things in the pictures, and enjoying all sorts of other fun, hands-on activities. The Bible will come alive for your child through these hands-on activities!

(Note: The handprints are there to help your child experience the story as he or she hears it. It may be helpful for some children to stop and do each activity at the spot indicated in the Bible passage, while other children may benefit from reading the story all the way through and then going back to do the activities later.)

Time to Pray and Let's Talk

Each passage ends with a prayer that makes the point of the Scripture personal. Discussion questions help you and your child discover how the Bible connects to your lives. Pray these prayers and discuss these questions with your child to help make your Bible reading meaningful. These are great ways for you and your child to interact with each other as you explore the meaning of the Scripture you've just read together.

Pockets and Cuddles

Your child will love how these adorable animals guide you both in making discoveries. Your child can easily find the prayer by looking for Pockets, the kangaroo. Likewise, Cuddles, the lamb, leads you and your child in the activities with each Bible story.

These fun characters give your child something familiar with each Bible story. Your child will look for Pockets and Cuddles in anticipation of fun learning.

To bring these recurring characters to your home, you can find Pockets and Cuddles puppets for sale at www.Group.com/MyHandsOnBible.

Activities

Each Bible story has two activities with it. These are simple activities, and many of them are things you can do as you go through your normal routines. These activities make it easy for you to make the Scripture a part of your child's life. They're a great way to review the story with your child the next day or later that week.

Read these on your own, and plan a time to lead your child through them. You may choose to do both of the activities or just one. Either way, each activity reinforces the Scripture to your child.

The Jesus Connection

Each passage ends with "The Jesus Connection." Your child will see that Jesus is the center of all Scripture, even passages that don't mention him. And your child will know that Jesus is a real part of life. So read these Jesus Connections to your child as a great way to show Jesus' presence in all of Scripture.

Thank you for choosing *God's Amazing Creation* for your child. God will use you to bring the Bible to life as you and your child go through it together!

God Creates

In the beginning
God created the
heavens and the earth.
2The earth was formless
and empty, and darkness
covered the deep waters.   And the
Spirit of God was hovering over the surface
of the waters.

"Cover your eyes for a few seconds and imagine what the earth was like."

3Then God said, "Let there be light," and
there was light. 4And God saw that the light
was good. Then he separated the light from the
darkness.

6Then God said, "Let there be a space

between the waters, to separate the waters of the heavens from the waters of the earth."

⁹Then God said, "Let the waters beneath the sky flow together into one place, so dry ground may appear." And that is what happened.

"Turn a light off and on as you say, 'Let there be light!'"

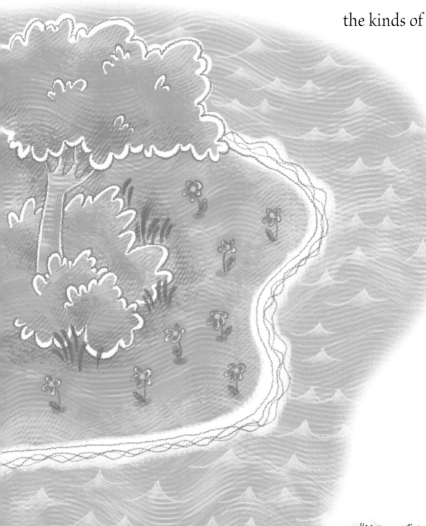

"Squat down like you're a little seed, then stand up like a tall tree."

¹⁰God called the dry ground "land" and the waters "seas." And God saw that it was good. ¹¹Then God said, "Let the land sprout with vegetation—every sort of seed-bearing plant, and trees that grow seed-bearing fruit. These seeds will then produce the kinds of

"Make a fish face."

plants and trees
from which they came."
And that is what happened.

¹⁶God made two great lights—the larger
one to govern the day, and the smaller one to
govern the night. He also made the stars.

²⁰Then God said, "Let the waters swarm
with fish and other life. Let the skies
be filled with birds of every kind." ²¹So God
created great sea creatures and every living
thing that scurries and swarms in the water,
and every sort of bird—each producing

"Let's draw a
sun and a moon.
Then let's sing
'Twinkle, Twinkle
Little Star.'"

13

offspring of the same kind. And God saw that it was good.

²⁵God made all sorts of wild animals, livestock, and small animals, each able to produce offspring of the same kind. And God saw that it was good.

"Act like your favorite animal."

THE
Jesus
CONNECTION   The Bible tells us

14

Let's Talk

- What's your favorite thing that God made?
- If you could change one thing that God made, what would it be?

Dear God, thank you for making such an amazing world for us. We love it—and we love you! In Jesus' name, amen.

Pockets says, "It's time to pray!"

Cloud Watching

Look at the sky this week to see if any clouds look like animal shapes to you. God made all those clouds—*and* every animal you can think of.

A New Creation

With your child, draw pretend animals. Then talk about the animals you made and the animals God made.

Cuddles says, "Let's get creative!"

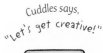

God created everything with his Son, Jesus.

"Look in a mirror at your image. God made us in his image!"

Then God said, "Let us make human beings in our image, to be like us. They will reign over the fish in the sea, the birds in the sky, the livestock, all the wild animals on the earth, and the small animals that scurry along the ground."

²⁷So God created human beings in his own

image. In the image of God he created them; male and female he created them.

²⁸Then God blessed them and said, "Be fruitful and multiply. Fill the earth and govern it. Reign over the fish in the sea, the birds in the sky, and all the animals that scurry along the ground."

"Pretend to swim like a fish, fly like a bird, and walk like an animal."

¹⁸Then the LORD God said, "It is not good for the man to be alone. I will make a helper who is just right for him." ¹⁹So the LORD God formed from the ground all the wild animals and all the birds of the sky. He brought them to the man to see what he would call them, and the man chose a name for each one. ²⁰He gave names to all the livestock, all the birds of the sky, and all the wild animals. But still there was no helper just right for him.

"If you had to call lions by a different name, what would it be? How about elephants?"

²¹So the LORD God caused the man to fall into a deep sleep.  While the man slept, the LORD God took out one of the man's ribs and closed up the opening. ²²Then the LORD God made a woman from the rib, and he brought her to the man.

²³"At last!" the man exclaimed.

"This one is bone from my bone, and flesh

"Make some snoring sounds!"

"Can you feel your ribs? How many can you count?"

19

from my flesh! She will be called 'woman,'
because she was taken from 'man.'"

²⁴This explains why a man leaves his father
and mother and is joined to his wife, and the
two are united into one.

THE Jesus CONNECTION

God made us in his image, but we are not exactly like God. Only Jesus is just like God!

Rhyme Time

Say this fun rhyme together, and do the motions in parentheses.

God made people, *(pound fists on top of each other)*
Both short and tall. *(crouch low, then stand up tall)*
God made people, *(pound fists on top of each other)*
He made them all! *(point outward and turn in a circle)*

People Plans

Make a person shape out of modeling dough. Talk about how God makes each person in your family special.

Let's Talk

• How can we take care of God's earth?
• What did God make special about you?

Dear God, you're amazing! Thank you for making us in your image so we are like you. In Jesus' name, amen.

Adam and

Genesis 3:1-7

"Pretend you're a snake. Can you move around without using your arms or legs?"

The serpent was the shrewdest of all the wild animals the LORD God had made. One day he asked the woman, "Did God really say you must not eat the fruit from any of the trees in the garden?"

"How many different kinds of fruit can you find on this page?"

²"Of course we may eat fruit from the trees in the garden," the woman replied. ³"It's only the fruit from the tree in the middle of the garden that we are not allowed to eat. God said, 'You

Eve's Sin

must not eat it or even touch it; if you do, you
will die.'"

⁴"You won't die!" the serpent replied to the
woman. ⁵"God knows that your eyes will be
opened as soon as you eat it, and you will be
like God, knowing both good and evil."

"Close your eyes,
and then open
them really big."

⁶The woman was convinced. She saw that the tree was beautiful and its fruit looked delicious, and she wanted the wisdom it would give her. So she took some of the fruit and ate it.

Then she gave some to her husband, who was with her, and he ate it, too. ⁷At that moment their eyes were opened, and they suddenly felt shame at their nakedness. So they sewed fig leaves together to cover themselves.

"Point to each different clothes item you're wearing."

Pockets says, *"It's time to pray!"*

Dear God, please help us to make good choices and do what's right when we have to choose between good and bad. In Jesus' name, amen.

Let's Talk

- What are some rules you have to follow?
- What happens when you don't obey the rules?
- What are some things you can do to obey God's rules?

THE Jesus CONNECTION

Plant Safari

Look for different kinds of plants with your child, including fruits, vegetables, and decorative plants. Help your child determine whether or not the plant can be eaten. Talk about how God's rules keep us safe.

Cuddles says,
"Let's find plants!"

House Rules

With your child, make a list of some of the rules in your house. At the end of the week, talk about which rules were hardest for your child to follow and why those rules are important.

Like Adam and Eve, we sometimes sin and feel bad.
The good news is that Jesus will always forgive us!

Noah

When Noah was 600 years old, on the seventeenth day of the second month, all the underground waters erupted from the earth, and the rain fell in mighty torrents from the sky. ¹²The rain continued to fall for forty days and forty nights.

¹³That very day Noah had gone into the boat with his wife and his sons—Shem, Ham, and Japheth—and their wives. ¹⁴With them in the boat were pairs of every kind of animal—domestic and wild, large and small—along

"Make rain sounds with me! First we'll rub our hands together, then clap them quietly, then clap them loudly, and then pat our hands on our legs."

with birds of every kind. ¹⁵Two by two they came into the boat, representing every living thing that breathes. ¹⁶A male and female of each kind entered, just as God had commanded Noah. Then the LORD closed the door behind them.

¹⁷For forty days the flood-waters grew

"Walk like an elephant, hop like a kangaroo, and run like a deer."

"What animals can you find on this page? What do they say?"

27

"Pretend you're in the big floating boat, sometimes called an ark, rocking back and forth."

deeper, covering the ground and lifting the boat high above the earth. [18] As the waters rose higher and higher above the ground, the boat floated safely on the surface. [19] Finally, the water covered even the highest mountains on the earth, [20] rising more than twenty-two feet above the highest peaks.

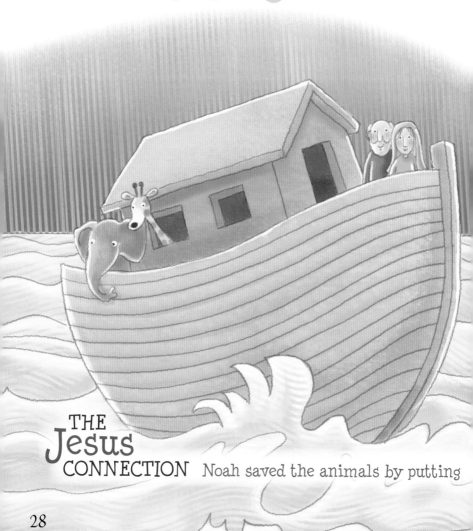

THE Jesus CONNECTION Noah saved the animals by putting

Pockets says, "It's time to pray!"

Dear God, we know you can help us do hard things like Noah did. Help us to trust you when hard things happen. In Jesus' name, amen.

Let's Talk

• What's something that's hard for you to do?
• How could God help you?

Safari

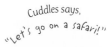

Cuddles says, "Let's go on a safari!"

This week, look for animals with your child, and talk about all the animals God kept safe on Noah's ark. Think of times when your family can trust God to keep you safe.

Tub Time

Give your child a plastic bowl to float in the tub as an ark. If you have small, waterproof animal toys, put them in the boat. Have your child make animal sounds and float the ark. Talk about how Noah trusted God in the ark and how we can trust God.

them on the ark. And God sent someone to save us—Jesus!

God's Rainbow Promise

Genesis 8–9

"Blow like the wind."

But God remembered Noah and all the wild animals and livestock with him in the boat. He sent a wind to blow across the earth, and the floodwaters began to recede.

⁸Then God told Noah and his sons, ⁹"I hereby confirm my covenant with you and your descendants, ¹⁰and with all the animals that were

"What colors do you
see in the picture
of a rainbow?"

on the boat with
you—the birds, the livestock,
and all the wild animals—
every living creature on earth.
¹¹Yes, I am confirming my
covenant with you. Never again
will floodwaters kill all living
creatures; never again will a flood
destroy the earth."

¹²Then God said, "I am giving you a sign
of my covenant with you and with all living
creatures, for all generations to come. ¹³I have
placed my rainbow in the clouds.   It is
the sign of my covenant with you and with
all the earth.   ¹⁴When I send clouds
over the earth, the rainbow
will appear in the clouds,
¹⁵and I will remember
my covenant with

"Make a rainbow
by putting your
fingers together."

31

you and with all living creatures. Never again will the floodwaters destroy all life. ¹⁶When I see the rainbow in the clouds, I will remember the eternal covenant between God and every living creature on earth." ¹⁷Then God said to Noah, "Yes, this rainbow is the sign of the covenant I am confirming with all the creatures on earth."

THE Jesus CONNECTION   Here's another promise

Shopping Search

Cuddles says, "Let's go shopping!"

While grocery shopping, have your child look for different colors on packaging. Whenever you check out, remind your child of the colors you saw and say, "God keeps his promises to all living creatures."

Rainbow Light

Hold a DVD shiny side up under a lamp, flashlight, or sunny window. Slowly move the DVD around to see the rainbow and identify its colors. Or create your own "rain" and rainbow outdoors with a fine spray from a hose. Talk about the promise God made and keeps today.

Let's Talk

• What's a promise you've made?
• Tell about a time someone kept a promise to you.

Pockets says, "It's time to pray!"

Dear God, thank you for making promises and keeping them. Thank you that you promise to always be with us. In Jesus' name, amen.

God made: he forgives us because Jesus died for our sins.

The Tower of Babel

Genesis 11:1-9

"The people moved to a new place. March around the room, then sit back down."

At one time all the people of the world spoke the same language and used the same words. ²As the people migrated to the east, they found a plain in the land of Babylonia and settled there.

³They began saying to each other, "Let's make

"Pretend to make some bricks! First pretend to scoop some clay and shape it. Then pat the bricks and stack them."

bricks and harden them with fire." (In this region bricks were used instead of stone, and tar was used for mortar.) ⁴Then they said, "Come, let's build a great city for ourselves with a tower that reaches into the sky. This will make us famous and keep us from being scattered all over the world."

⁵But the LORD came down to look at the city and the tower the people were building. ⁶"Look!" he said. "The

"Reach as high as you can!"

"Count to three in Spanish! Uno, dos, tres."

people are united, and they all speak the same language. After this, nothing they set out to do will be impossible for them! ⁷Come, let's go down and confuse the people with different languages. Then they won't be able to understand each other." ⁸In that way, the LORD scattered them all over the world, and they stopped building the city. ⁹That is why the city was called Babel, because that is where the LORD confused the people with different languages. In this way he scattered them all over the world.

"Pretend you're people who are scattering to places all over the world! Run to whatever place I point to."

THE Jesus CONNECTION The people in the Bible

Pockets says,
"It's time to pray!"

Dear God, sometimes we think we can do whatever we want without your help. Please teach us to ask for your help to do what pleases you. In Jesus' name, amen.

Tower Power

Have your child try to build a block tower up to the ceiling without any help. As he or she builds the tower that eventually falls or can't be completed, discuss how the people in the Bible were proud and thought they didn't need God's help. Talk about why it's important to ask God to help us.

Foreign Foods

Cuddles says,
"Let's eat new food!"

For one meal this week, have your family's favorite ethnic food. Talk about ways your country is different from other countries. Pray that people from different countries will learn that God loves them.

Let's Talk

• What do you like to do all by yourself?
• What can God help you with this week?

ouldn't get to God by building a tall tower. But we can be close to God by trusting Jesus to forgive our sins.

God's Promise

"Count as many stars as you can on this page."

Then the LORD took Abram outside and said to him, "Look up into the sky and count the stars if you can. That's how many descendants you will have!"

¹When Abram was ninety-nine years old, the LORD appeared to him and said, "I am El-Shaddai—'God Almighty.' Serve me faithfully and live a blameless life. ²I will make a covenant with you, by which I will guarantee to give you countless descendants."

38

to Abraham

"Lay with your face down like Abram did."

³At this, Abram fell face down on the ground. Then God said to him, ⁴"This is my covenant with you: I will make you the father of a multitude of nations! ⁵What's more, I am changing your name. It will no longer be Abram. Instead, you will be called Abraham, for you will be the father of many nations.

"Say your full name."

"God promised to love Abraham's family and to make it a big family. Name some people you know who love God. They all belong to Abraham's family!"

⁶I will make you extremely fruitful. Your descendants will become many nations, and kings will be among them!

⁷"I will confirm my covenant with you and your descendants after you, from generation to generation. This is the everlasting covenant: I will always be your God and the God of your descendants after you."

Pockets says, "It's time to pray!"

Dear God, thank you for keeping your promise to love Abraham and his family. Help us to love you and trust you, just like Abraham did. In Jesus' name, amen.

Let's Talk

• What do people do to show they love you?
• What does God do to show he loves you?

THE Jesus CONNECTION

Promise Cheer

Repeat this cheer with your child while you're driving or walking somewhere this week:

**Promises, promises,
God keeps his promises!
God keeps his promise
to love me
(help me,
forgive me,
teach me)!**

Cuddles says,
"Let's cheer!"

Uncountable Stars

On a clear night, take your family outside, and have your child try to count as many stars as possible. Talk about how God promised Abraham as many grandkids as there are stars—and that he promised to love them.

God kept his promise to Abraham. And God will keep his promise to us that we can go to heaven if we believe in Jesus.

Isaac

The LORD
kept his word and did for
Sarah exactly what he had promised. ²She
became pregnant, and she gave birth to a son
for Abraham in his old age. This happened
at just the time God had said it would.

"Grab a doll or
stuffed animal
and hold it like
you would hold
a baby."

42

Is Born

Genesis 21:1-7

³And Abraham named their son Isaac. ⁴Eight days after Isaac was born, Abraham circumcised him as God had commanded. ⁵Abraham was 100 years old when Isaac was born.

⁶And Sarah declared, "God has brought me laughter. All who hear about this will laugh with me.

"Clap your hands 100 times."

[7]Who would have said to Abraham that Sarah would nurse a baby? Yet I have given Abraham a son in his old age!"

"Sarah laughed because she was happy. Let out a really happy laugh."

THE Jesus CONNECTION God gave us the best gift when he

Pockets says,
"It's time to pray!"

Dear God, you gave Sarah a baby, and that made her very happy. Help us to be happy and say thank you when you give us good gifts. In Jesus' name, amen.

Let's Talk

• What are some of the best things God has given you?
• What are some things you want God to give you?

Beautiful Babies

Cuddles says,
"Let's find babies!"

Look for babies this week. Whenever your child sees a baby, talk with your child about God's gift to Sarah. And talk about things God has given you.

Gifts from God

With your child, collect several things around the house that are gifts from God. Talk about how each thing is a gift from God, and thank him for each gift you've collected.

gave us Jesus, who loves us, helps us, and forgives us.

Special Bible Verses to Remember

In the beginning God created the heavens and the earth.
Genesis 1:1

I am with you, and I will protect you wherever you go.
Genesis 28:15

The heavens proclaim the glory of God.
Psalm 19:1

The Lord is my shepherd; I have all that I need.
Psalm 23:1

This is the day the Lord has made. We will rejoice and be glad in it.
Psalm 118:24

Our help is from the Lord, who made heaven and earth.
Psalm 124:8

Thank you for making me so wonderfully complex!
Psalm 139:14

Every word of God proves true. He is a shield to all who come to him for protection.

Proverbs 30:5

I will strengthen you and help you.

Isaiah 41:10

Do not be afraid, for I am with you.

Isaiah 43:5

Love your neighbor as yourself.

Matthew 22:39

For God loved the world so much that he gave his one and only Son, so that everyone who believes in him will not perish but have eternal life.

John 3:16

Whatever you do, do it all for the glory of God.

1 Corinthians 10:31

I can do everything through Christ, who gives me strength.

Philippians 4:13

Tape or glue a photo of your family on this page.
Remember to pray for your family members every day!